Cattitudes

In memory of my beloved pets,
Abbie and Buster.

JRP

Cattitudes

A Collection of Cattiverse
by
J R Poulter

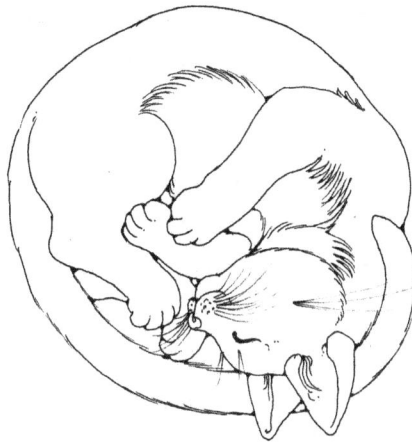

Illustrated
by
Dandi Palmer

Word Wings
Books

National Library of Australia Cataloguing-in-Publication entry

Creator: Poulter, J. R., author.

Title: Cattitudes: a collection of cattiverse/J.R. Poulter ; illustrator/designer,
Dandi Palmer.

ISBN: 9781925484281 (paperback)

Notes: Includes bibliographical references.

Subjects: Cats--Poetry.
Pets--Poetry.
Australian poetry.

Other Creators/Contributors: Palmer, Dandi, illustrator, book designer.

Dewey Number: A821.4

CONTENTS

The Perrrfect Pet!

i) Cat Caller

G'day Matt,
So you're off!
A favour? Sure thing!
Care of your pet,
A companionable cat?
I can handle that,
I like cats!

Now -
How long are you going?
Mmmmmm,
There's no way of knowing -
But you *will* be back?
Might be a while down the
track -
Don't mean to sound rude, but
Money for food?
No, well…of course,
Not like minding a horse!
No worries about that,
So there's plenty of food,
Uncle left you a ranch…
WOW!

Mmmmmm
Hope you don't mind my asking
But just 'xactly how
Big is this cat?
He lives in your flat…
Well, yeah, sure!
Your kitty will have good home
Even take him out country
When he wants to roam!
So, when? Saturday -
Bring him on over then Matt!
Oh, yeah and
What's the name of your cat?
JAWS!

1

ii) Cat Carer

Mrs Jones it's WAY early
A quarter past three!
Saturdays I sleep in -
Turn down your TV,
I can't hear for the din!
It's not the TV...
It's your children all screaming.
Well don't feed them tripe
And then they'll stop dreaming -
Whooo -
Settle down petal!
I wasn't being rude,
But kids don't have nightmares
When fed 'normal' food!

SLAM!

One narky neighbour!
Just what is her beef!
The things people fuss for's
Just way beyond belief!
I'm going back to bed,
I really need sleep!
Today Matt brings his cat,
Must be ready for that....

ROARRRRGH!

Now what's all that noise?
It's a bit hard to see out -
I'll put on the light.

CLICK!

What's the shouting
about?!

ROAR!

AWWWWW –
Look at those teeth!
Matt?
THIS is the cat?!

2

The Nationalities of Cats

White cats are queens on cushions with cream,
Dreaming of fishing eternal streams,
Wishing for dishes like pigeon pie
And how a cat might learn to fly
And chase the birds across the sky!

Tabbies are tigers who blend with the rushes,
Slipping like shadows from under the bushes,
Liquid in motion they pass,
Like wind gliding over the grass!

The Siamese sit with their eyes wary slits
Stalking their servant and master.
Their due is the homage of choicest titbits,
No cat is sleeker or faster!

Piebald cats are clowns and tumblers
With wicked grins and jaunty airs
Sauntering backyards and alleys,
Catch as catch can who dares!

But the black cat's the creature of legend and myth
Who lives by both stealth and his wiles.
He appears out of nowhere and sits by your fire
When you ask, "Where've you been?" he just smiles.

Of Catalumphs and Hippograffes

Catalumph and Hippograffe
Went out to take some tea,
Said Catalumph to Hippograffe,
"You walk too slow, dear,
Don't you know,
You must catch up with me!"

Said Hippograffe to Catalumph,
"My dear, it's very plain,
Your legs are long and mine are short,
With every step you gain!"
So,
Catalumph walked and Hippograffe ran
And they arrived on time, as planned.

Cat Character No. 1. - Mes Feline

I have a cat in a bowler hat
Who struts his stuff in style!
He went to dine at *Le Chez Feline*
And ordered jalapos and wine.

The wine was fine but the chilli was hot,
Hot as pepper from the pot!
The cat spat the chilli back into the vat,
Threw up in his bowler hat,
Was booted out onto the welcome mat.

A sorry cat with a ruined hat,
He sadly sat under the new neon sign
Drank the rest of the bottle of wine
And that was that for Mes Feline!

Cat Character No. 2 - Abbie

Silver tabby,
Cryptic minx,
Who knows just what
That cat thinks!

She purrs, paws
With sheathed claws,
Minx!

Crouched in the shadows,
Mysterious sphinx,
Waits till the moment
The sun finally sinks
Then glides down the darkness
Past where the moon winks!

Slink, slink,
Bright eyes stare -
What's there?

Poised for action…
POUNCE!
Reaction -
Big eyes blink,
It's just a skink!

Cat Character No 3 ~ Buster Fiddez

Tuxedo and spats
But where's your top hat,
Mr Cat?

Festival mask,
Where's he off to?
I ask.

He's darting the dark
Down the alleys
To park,

He's under the fence
Where the foliage
Is dense,

Can you see him now?
Can you hear him
Meow?

Yowwwwwwwl!
Mr Cat's on
The prowl!

Cat Character No 4 - A Tabby

Abbie's just an
Average tabby
To anyone
Just passing by.
Stop a moment,
Take a look.
Those eyes are full
As story books,
Old cat wise …

Domesticated

Gliding, a shadow among shades,
the grey she-cat among the shrubbery,
sliding down the darkness,
crouching on the wall -
leaves no softer fall,
no sound at all...
Pause, poised,
LEAP!
A flutter and a shriek!

This was an exercise of ancient will.
Well fed,
the grey cat practises
the kill.

Lady Elise and the Tiger!

Once on my travels, I came to the Niger
And there heard a story, just a tad gory,
Of Lady Elise who walked with a tiger,
Walked by the Niger, a tiger beside her!
The lady had hired the tiger to guide her.

The tiger, called Sheba, had her own agenda,
To dine on the lady and, not to offend her,
Spun Lady Elise a most fanciful tale!

But the glint in her eye made the lady turn pale.
"Come now," smiled Sheba, "It's not very far."
But she thought to herself, 'What a silly you are,
For into my jungle lair I will guide you.'

"Soon," said the tiger, "You'll not need me beside you!"
'No doubt,' thought Elise, 'for I'll be inside you!'
Lady Elise, having hired her the tiger
To guide her along the banks of the Niger,
Said to herself, 'What have I acquired here?
Something quite dire is what is required here!
I think I'll feign tired and insist that I ride her!'

Now as anyone knows, any lady who goes
For a walk by the Niger, a tiger beside her,
Is a curious sight. But what's sure to delight
And draw news reporters from far, far and wider
Is a tiger with lady sat quaintly astride her
Riding along the banks of the Niger.

Tigers, vain creatures as everyone knows,
Never lose them a chance for striking a pose!
And so our fair lady who hired her a tiger
To guide her the length of the wild River Niger,
Arrived at her depot astride the large tiger
Accompanied by cameramen, journos, reporters,
Who snapped and asked questions, just as they ought to.

But the lady, as ladies of quality do,
Was due for a headache. It came right on cue!
Said Elise to the tiger, "Now do be a dear,
And rid me of all that flashlighting gear,
And the noise of those journos, it's more'n I can bear!"

Said the tiger, "Why lady, I'll offer to guide 'em,
Along the wild Niger they may walk beside me,
But once in my lair, why they'll rumble inside me!"
Now journos aren't silly, they can read lips,
And when they kenned Sheba saw them as tidbits,
They took off in a zillion directions at once,
Except for Elise, and she was no dunce!

Quick as a whisker, she knew what to do
She leapt back on Sheba and rode to the Zoo!
They rode to the Zoo, to the tiger, all new.
This looked like pre-packaged come-help-yourself food!
The tiger, though wary, wasn't up to their tricks.
One moment she halted and, quick as a flick,
The Zookeeper threw one net and then two!

Our Tiger became a creature of fame!
They even had the Zoo renamed
To honour the day that Sheba came!
Now the moral is plain, but I'll say it again,
Always ride ASTRIDE tigers, who AREN'T eating you,
Particularly touring the banks of the Niger
Conducted by tour-guides
With teeth like a TIGER'S!

Pleas to Please!

How do you please a cat?
Do you ever take time to consider the fact
That cats
Need to be pleased
And never, no never,
That's not even EVER,
Be teased!

Pat a cat,
Scratch a cat!
Just like that -
Under the ear,
Under the chin!
Watch them grin!
Stroke their fur,
Hear them purrrrrrr...

Play with your cat,
Day or night they like that.
Trail a thing on a string,
Roll a ball.
That's all!
Cats are easy to please!
Except
With their meals...

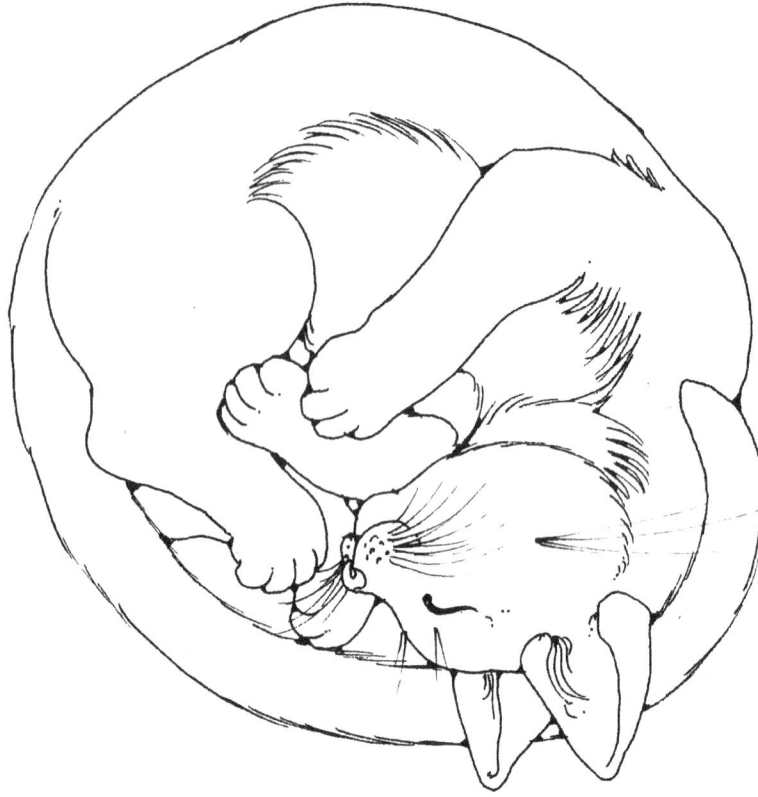

Cat Curl

Cat,
Curl cuddled on my lap,
What
Would you do
If hunting were your lot
And not
Merely a way to pass
Time for a sublimely
Leisured class?

Lean Cat Cuisine

Late afternoon
The little cats come,
The licketty split, thin as a stick
Cats
Peering and staring from under the bushes
Wary and waiting
For the last tides of late folk
To go,
Leaving them be,
Lords and Ladies,
To pick at the bins
The happy scraps, lush for licking, nice nibbly bits
That tickle the tongue!
The elegant cats'
Lean feline cuisine -
Burger bits, gravied chips, a bit o bun, fried rice -
Nice -
Mmmmm this's **YUM!**

Living Dangerously

We have a pair, pet lady rats,
And one pet cat.
The rats live in a spacious cage
That's safe by any person's gauge.

"What are you doing Miss Pusscat?"
 "Me?-owww!"
"I don't think the rats
Are at all convinced
That your intents are innocent!"
  "ME?!-owww!"

Wood and wire, the cage is stout!
It keeps Miss Puss, the hunter, out.
But Jingles and Abigail tremble with fear
'Cause 'Scent of Pusscat' lingers there.

"What are you doing Miss Pusscat?"
 "ME?!-owww?!"
"You prowl and growl
And sharpen your claws
And smile so they see
All the teeth in your jaws!"
 "Meee?-owww...."

"Would you be brave
If lions roamed our street
And you weren't convinced
They'd enough to eat?
So how'd THAT be Pusscat?!"
 "Me - OWWWWW!"

Take a Back Seat!

The bus stank of cat pee, boy was it RANK!
And I wasn't sure why till I moved down the aisle
And saw sprawled out on the very back seat
A cat, a BIG CAT with a very BIG smile…
It looked like the tiger I dreamed of last night
But I stood there stock still like my shoes'd been glued
While my mental amenities quitted me quite!

This tiger yawned, stretched and flexed his long claws
I couldn't help noting the TEETH in those JAWS!
I knew, if he wanted, I'd be gone in one bite,
It was then I remembered, with tigers, don't flinch,
Don't move a muscle or falter an inch
Stand still, or play dead, don't register fright,
And they're bound to get bored.

Trouble was, whilst determinedly getting ignored,
I recalled I'm allergic to cats!
Could there ever be a more irksome curse
Than fixing a tiger with watering eyes
And nose itching and twitching and worse!
I strained and I stressed till I just couldn't bear it…
I SNEEZED! But
There'd been no need to fear it!
The tiger, he lifted four feet in the air
And his stripes…. Oh cripes!
They rained down like liquorice strips into my hair!

18

Cat Factorium

What do you wish?
Is it fresh fish?
What cat
Could resist that?
But no...
First things first
Nothing can match
A timely scratch!

In the Shadow of the Heart

Hush!   Listen -
Something   is crying in
The night at the   edge of a dream,
Inanimate as the heart between each beat.
Something draws to windows within the eyes.
You know the cry, you've heard it before.
You picture - the bird and the black cat -
A creature hunched against the dark,
A preying figure in the shadow,
Walls climbing down round
Till the dark's so close,
Hammering hard
At the window,
It holds the
Heart's
Beat

-

RAAAAHHHHRRRR!

Baby Lion threw a tantrum,
Flipped his food onto the floor,
Rubbed mashed banana through
Brother's hair,
And pinched till he was sore!
Father Lion just sat there,
But Mother Lion went, "Roar!"

Baby Lion tossed toys about,
His clothes all ripped and tore,
Refused to have his bath and
Pinched his Brother more!
Father Lion just sat there,
But Mother Lion went, "ROAR!"

Baby lion pulled faces
When they all went to the store,
Dumped icecream in a lady's lap
Which he blamed his Brother for!
Father Lion just stood there,
But Mother Lion went, "roar!"

Sawed Father's chair through with the saw,
Fished in the loo with Father's false teeth,
Scratched Brother with his paw!
Mother Lion just sat there,
But Father Lion went, "ROAR!"

Baby Lion took Brother's favourite toy,
Ate his apple and left him the core,
Broke the head off his GI Joe,
And whacked him in the jaw!
Father Lion just sat there,
Mother Lion went, "R O A R! !"

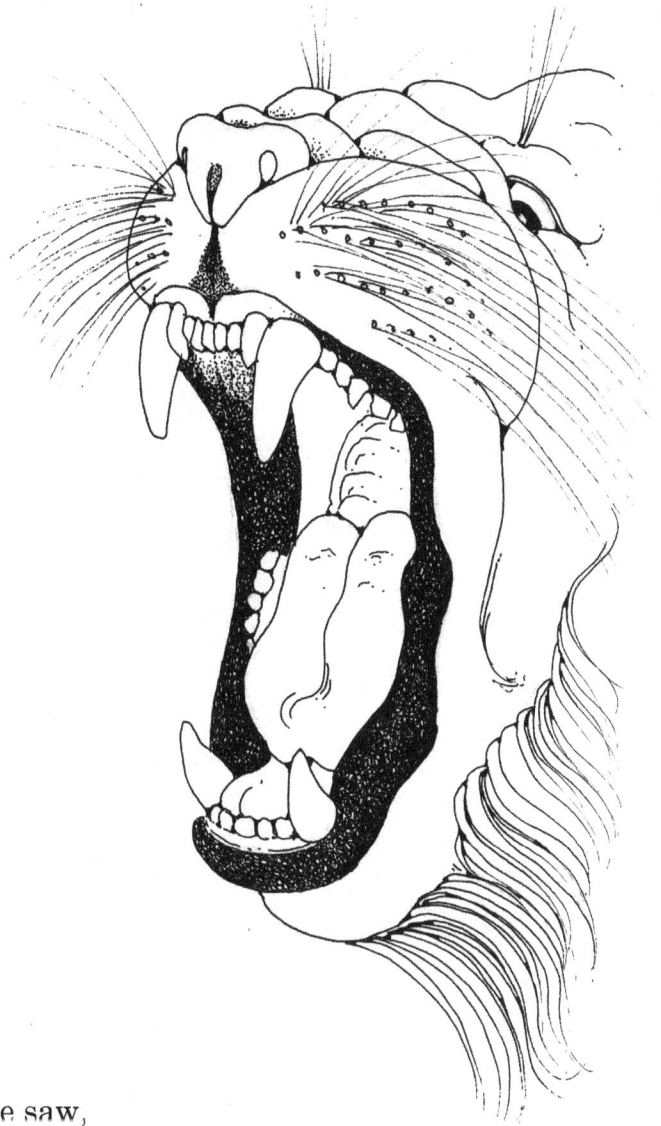

But Brother cried, "You little rat!"
He'd really had enough of that
And, with one great almighty <u>ROOAARRRR</u>,
He stormed out the room
And slammed the door!

Does Bro' love Baby Brother?
In twelve months here's the score,
They're running round and kicking ball!
They're best of mates for sure!

RAAAAHHHHRRRR!

One Dog and Two Cats
(for Merry's Sarah)

Oh, so you're home?
About time too!
Come and see what
I've got
To show you!
That cat of yours,
He's killed a bird,
And I barked and barked
But not a word
From cat No.2.
She took his side.

Come and see quick!

I have SUCH a job
Keeping your mini pride in line
And aren't I a good girl!
Pat me again.
Scratch me there,
Behind the ear -
Ah, yes - you approve.
I love you too.

23

Her Majesty's Adviser

I am the second oldest kit of Cat McGonaggel.
My pelt's pure black, bar down my back
Stipples of whitest fur.
I am the Queen of Scotland's Cat.
I curl on her throne in her old fur hat
And purr.
And she defers to me above
The grey and crinkled men of her wrinkled ministry.
She listens to their monotones
Then dismisses them in superior tones.
Now cat, she says when we're alone,
We will do that, or this, or what
Do you think we should do with that lot?
I look up at her and blink,
And she says, *I know! That's what I think!*
And so it goes and nobody knows
Just what transpires in the blink of an eye
Between the Queen
And I!

CATastrophe!

Cats
Do NOT friend RATS!
That's that!

So why Missy Molly
This terrible folly?!

This morning,
A whisker past dawning ,
I spied you being chatty
In modes most uncatty
With one little ratty!
Tut tut!

You just sat
Nose to nose with a rat,
No scatting or spatting,
Just sitting there chatting!

The whole so unseeming,
I thought I was dreaming.
"This can't be," I said
And I went back to bed.

No sooner did I shut my eyes
Than skitter noises start to rise.
It's way too early in the day
For next door's kids
Being out to play.
I crawled to the door.
Can you guess what I saw?

My cat with a rat!
My jolly Miss Molly
Spread flat on our mat
And that rat!
They were
Tête–à–tête,
A rat and my pet
In a Meow Powwow
Talking squeak
Speak!

EEK FREAK!

I took my cat to the local vet.
He told me not to fuss and fret.
He said
To take a sedative
And take myself to bed.

I don't think he believed me.
I think it most unfair.
I'm perfectly adjusted,
My cat's the one that's weird!

My cat is sitting all agog
In 'deep and meaning' with a DOG!
Cats and dogs just do not stroll
And let the conversation roll.
They don't step out, don't go for walks
And pass their time in idle talks.
Cats DO NOT share
Their deepest care
With canine critters ANYWHERE.

The 'normal' for a dog and cat
Is VERY LOUD and spit 'n spat.

I took my cat down to the zoo,
I did not know what else to do!
He had the most amazing time,
His conversations were sublime
With alligator, kangaroo,
A zebra, cheetah and baboon,
A possum, rhino and raccoon.

I was supremely confident,
I was, in fact, quite sure,
At last my cat was all talked out,
I had achieved a cure!

When I awoke this morning,
Still stretching and still yawning,
I saw the most distressing scene
A cat owner could ever see.
I'm seriously thinking of moving house -
My cat was talking to a MOUSE!

I thought of sending Miss Molly to sea,
Or to a dairy farm, but she
Stood up on her hind legs, looked me in the eye
And said with a sigh,
"You talk to your neighbour in Singhalese.
You had Chinese for tea last night.
You read in French as well as write,
So why shouldn't I try and follow your lead?
You humans are an intolerant breed!"

Walking Mr. Cat!

I took my cat out for a walk.
I didn't know that it would rain.
Now Aunt says I must carry him
All the way home again!

It wouldn't be so bad except
He doesn't like the wet.
He wiggles round and fusses so
And mewls and meows and frets!

It's like I have to carry
A bag of angry worms!
I'm glad my coat is good and thick
He scratches when he squirms!

Tempting morsels!

I know I'm not supposed to get
My paws and maw completely wet
By dipping them in this Goldfish bowl
And yet
My people must know
It tempts me so
To see this tasty dinner swim
Just paw's length below
The fish bowl's rim!

King Cat and His Bride!

Narrator: The King of all the Feline Beasts
   And Queen of Birds of Prey
   Are holding them a wedding feast
   Upon a certain day.
   The servants are preparing.
   The kitchen staff are trained.
   Just no one is to mention 'bird'.
   The Butler will explain…

Butler: Hoskins, the menu,
   You must get this right!
   The feast for the beasts
   And the birds is tonight!

Servant: What meal would appeal
   To the King of the Cats
   Do you think that it's eel?
   Does he wish for a dish
   Of fish, fish, fish, fish?
   Pâté of parrot, fillet of finch,
   Consommé of cockatiel
   Should be a cinch!

Butler: Now Hoskins REMEMBER,
   Just DO NOT forget
   NOT a word about 'BIRD'!
   That's a MUST! Are you set?
   No mention of poultry,
   No mention of fowl,
   'Bird' is a word
   That MUST NOT be heard!
   Do I have your ear,
   Is that PERFECTLY clear?

Servant: What?
 No finger lickin' chicken
 No plump pigeon pie
 No quail in quiche
 Nor duck and peach
 Or goose in batter fried?

Narrator: Is he hard of hearing?
 No savvy at all?!

Butler: Now Hoskins recall
 All I've told you -
 Not a word about 'bird'!
 Do listen! Hoskins Attend!
 NO word about bird!

Servant: Well then,
 Is whiting in white wine
 A dish to his liking
 Or pike?
 Or hake lightly baked
 With sauce of course!
 Is it bream for him, Sir
 And what about her, Sir,
 Must she also eat fish?
 Her majesty may not wish fish as a dish.
 So - what about mice?
 They're very nice
 Served on a bed of steamed white rice
 That's subtly spiced!

Butler: Ah, yes!
 That should suit the feline taste
 Especially with a rodent baste!
 A morsel of mouse as an entrée sits nicely
 With a main dish of fish!
 What more could King Cat and his lady Queen wish!
 Now hurry up, sirrah,
 You must keep the King happy,
 Do be a good chappy,

 Go snap up a snapper
 And, yes, the mice, a kilo or two,
 That should do!
 If King Cat gets too hungry,
 If you know what I mean,
 He might become partial to a portion of Queen!

Servant: Oh sir now I see
        Why some words
        Are unheard
        In the palace of Catkin!
        I mustn't say bird,
        I know it's absurd,
        But the Queen is an owl
        And they're FOWL
        Sorts of birds!!

Narrator: It's now a little later,
        A modicum of time ...
        All should be at ready,
        There goes the dinner chime...!

Butler: Ah, you there, Hoskins!
        The table is set.
        Is everyone greeted
        And seated as yet?
        Is cook all prepared
        With no expense spared,
        An elaborate fare
        For our right royal pair?

Servant: A trout for the King!
        The very thing!
        Next dish they'll bring -
        Fat rats
        For the courtier cats!
        A dish of voles
        And sautéed moles!
        Spiced mice
        For the Queen!
        Oh look at her preen!
        Her cousin Sir Hawk
        Is having a gawk
        At a rare bit of rabbit.
        Oh darn and dagnabbit,
        What FOUL eating habits!
        Ummmm....

Narrator: Well that was unsubtle...

Butler: Horrors! Hoskins!
        What WERE you thinking?!
        There's no excuse,
        Unless you've been drinking?
        If I were you,
        I'd beat a retreat
        Before Birds take wing
        And Cats get to their feet
        And decide bird AND human
        Just might be a TREAT!

Tilly and Trixie

I live in the penthouse,
She lives in the mews.
She gets all the gossip.
I get all the news.

Together we saunter
The back lanes and alleys
When owners are sleeping
And night critters sally.

No one suspects,
We have other lives.
Nobody knows
But Tilly and I,
Just what it takes
For a cat to survive!

Everyone's Cats and Someone

Prowling the perimeters, somewhere out of mind,
Are the streamline predators, feline kind.

Slink, slink, slink, s-s-s-t-r-e-t-c-h long and lean,
All sinew and muscle and eyes peeled keen!

"Where've you been?
Let me tell you what I've seen!
Down on the corner underneath the tree,
Mistress Moon-Eye, Lynx and ME
Waiting for something, what could it be?!!"

On the first of If Ever,
In the year of Zin,
Cats go out
And Dogs come in!

Cats sniff and scuffle and spat and sing.
Cats scat about, do the scouting thing.
MREOWWWWWWW!

On the last day of Whenever,
In the year of Zin,
Dogs back out
And Cats are in.

How did all of this begin?

Someone in Somewhere
Out back of the night
Heard all the screeching,
The yowling and fight,
Said, "This,
All this hiss
And spitting
And fits
Of scritching and scratching and
Flying furry bits,
It must stop!"

Said Someone, "I want to get some sleep,
Somewhere in the night dark deep!"

But Everyone else in the wide world complained,
"It's not fair the kittens and cats get blamed!
It's the dogs, it's the dogs,
They howl and howl,
Barking and yapping
And yowl upon yowl!
All this wolfing and prowling
The moonlight hours down
Is stealing the wee hours
Where we store our day powers!
We don't want them round!"

That's how,
In the midst of For Ever,
In the year of Zin,
Dogs go out
And cats come in!

"Hey you out back
In the junk yard pack!
It's our turn now
To stir and row!
YOWWWWWWWW
OW OW OW OWWWWWWW!"

The Sea Cat Dreams

I sit in the sun on the window sill,
Beyond the window, the sea.
It waves its white fingers, "Remember,
Remember," it murmurs to me.

I love the taste of salt sea breath
And sea surge distant moan.
I was not born a sailor's cat,
I am, now I am grown.

I was born on a farm with a cherry tree,
Where the blossoms fluttered and flew.
I played with the pup and the farmer's child,
Together we romped and grew!

I remember the noise of farmyard geese,
The shush of ducks curled in their feathers.
I recall the raven on the wall,
And the butterflies' dance together.

Then came a traveller with haversack,
Who smelled of herring fish.
He stayed a night by the firelight
And left with a heave and a swish!

I snuggled deep in his salty sack
Adrift with dreams of sea.
Not till his sack was stowed aboard
Did the sailor man find me!

The sailor, the cook and the captain all
Welcomed me on as crew.
I chased the rats in the cargo hold.
That earned me all my due!

I sat on deck whilst dolphins played,
Skimming and racing beside,
A leap and a splash, they were gone in a flash,
Where the ocean rolls deep and wide...

There came a storm and my sailor
Was swept from the deck to the sea.
They searched for days in its vastness.
Then I meowed his eulogy.

They gave me to his grieving wife
In her cottage alone on the shore.
I'm a comfort to her and she cares for me.
What could I ask for more!

Now I curl under wind blown curtains
To the whisper of waves and foam.
I dream of the sea, the dolphins, the man.
I wake to the salt scent of home...

SCAREDY WHO?!

Kitty Kins, Catty Kins minding the keep
Whilst the soldiers and sentries are all fast asleep,
What is that coming
Creep, c-r-e-e-p-i-l-y creep
Up from the moat where the bank is less steep?

CHORUS:
Squeak, SQUEEEEEAK
It's the scullery mice downstairs
Whoooo HOOO
It's the owls up there in the trees.
Creak SCREEEK
It's rusty hinges in the wind
BooHoo Cooo Cooo
It's only the pigeons high in the eaves.
Then Who????

What is it coming so stealthy and sly
With nary a sound but the night breeze's sigh?
Closer it comes! Now it's over the wall!
Hushhhhhh... Did you hear that?
No. Nothing at all...

What shall we do?
I'm scared, are you?
I wonder if maybe
It's scared too?
Whoooo... Whoooo...

What is it peeping round corners and doors,
Creeping on flippers, on feet or on paws,
Or something I know not that's down on all fours!?
What is it? Shadow flit down in the dark unlit
Crawling round crevices, crouching in nooks?
Kitty Kins, Catty Kins, shall we go look?!

Then who who who
Shall we go and see?
Who Who WHO
Shall we just let it be?
WHOOOOOOO WHOOOOOOO.......

Quick, run in the shadows,
Run under the eaves,
Run down the pathway
And brush past the leaves!
Hurry up, hurry up, hurry up do!
Something is hurrying,
Something is scurrying
Fast after me, after you!
HURRY DO!

Kitty Kins, Catty Kins
In through the door,
Don't pause a moment,
Not one second more!
Hurry up Kitty Cat
Leave, leave, leave, LEAVE!
Over the threshold...
Shove, push and heave –
Oh no, it is jammed!
WHAM! We have shut it?
BAM! It is slammed!
WHEEEEEEW!
What's that noise in the corner?
That ... you?

41

Funny Bones!

Funny Bones, kitten,
Listen up do!
Don't lie by the fire
When the cauldron's a-stew
Because dragons are stirring,
Their golden throats burning,
Down in the dungeons
They smell the strong brew!

Kitten Bones, listen,
Don't lie by the fire,
Curled up in a ball.
They won't see 'cat' at all,
Just another black dot
Like the black cooking pot!

Funny Bones cat,
Don't lie there like that!
Listen kitten, listen...
The dragons are stirring,
Their golden throats burning,
They're flying up from the caverns,
They're flying from the caves,
The crypts and the dungeons
Their cravings to stave!

The dragons are coming!
Oh kitten be quick!
Don't pause for a casual
Scratch or a lick!
THEY'RE COMING! THEY'RE
COMING!
The aroma is heady!
Can't you hear their wings flapping?
They KNOW the brew's ready!

OH KITTEN DO LISTEN!
NOW Funny Bones, PLEASE!
You give me conniptions,
You seem so at ease
When the dragons ARE coming,
You can hear their throats roar,
Soon they'll soar through the window,
They'll pour through the door!
OH KITTEN, DO LISTEN!
NOW! Funny Bones, NOW!

WHACK!

Well that was effective!
So why did I worry?!
A dragon's no match for a cat
In no hurry!

Mistress Mouse

"Oh, Missy Mouse, it is hot in the sun
And your brolla's such a natty one
With rainbow colors, flair and style!
May I shelter there a little while?"

"Well, Mr. Cat,
You flatter me
But it's just a wee brolla,
As you can see."

"Oh come, Missy Mouse,
You're sleek and fine,
Come walk with me
We'll go and dine!"

With that Miss Mouse,
At the mention of 'dine,'
Made a dash for her house
And just made it in time!

This tale has a moral,
It's best to be wise,
Be wary of folk
In a flatterer's guise!

Good Reasons for Having a Cat

1.
There's a mouse in the house
Or maybe two...
Perhaps there's a few?
Wait a bit! What was that?
I think I might have to
Invest in a cat!

2.
I have a problem with the milk.
I always have too much.
I like to have it fresh each day
But left over bottles just
Get in the way
And sour milk's such
An awful smell!
A cat, in fact,
Might do rather well...
Add to grocery list a note -
Buy one cat with creamy coat!

3.
Grandfather is getting old.
Old people's toes get rather cold.
Cats love to curl up on beds 'n purr
And have the warmest softest fur!
If I buy my cold, old Gramps a cat
That'll take care of that!

4.
My Aunt Patrice
Is ill at ease.
She has persistent callers.
They come at two
And leave at four
But not before
They eat the cakes
That she has baked.
It leaves her rather sore!

Because she is my favourite aunt,
I said to her "They really can't
Keep eating all the cakes you make!"

I rounded up the village strays
And brought them round to her each day.
We arrive on queue
At a quarter to two
And sit on all her parlour chairs.

When Aunt's freeloading friends appear,
Aunt answers the door with,
"Dear, oh dear,
I don't have spare chairs anywhere...
So very sorry to disappoint,
I hope your noses aren't out of joint!"

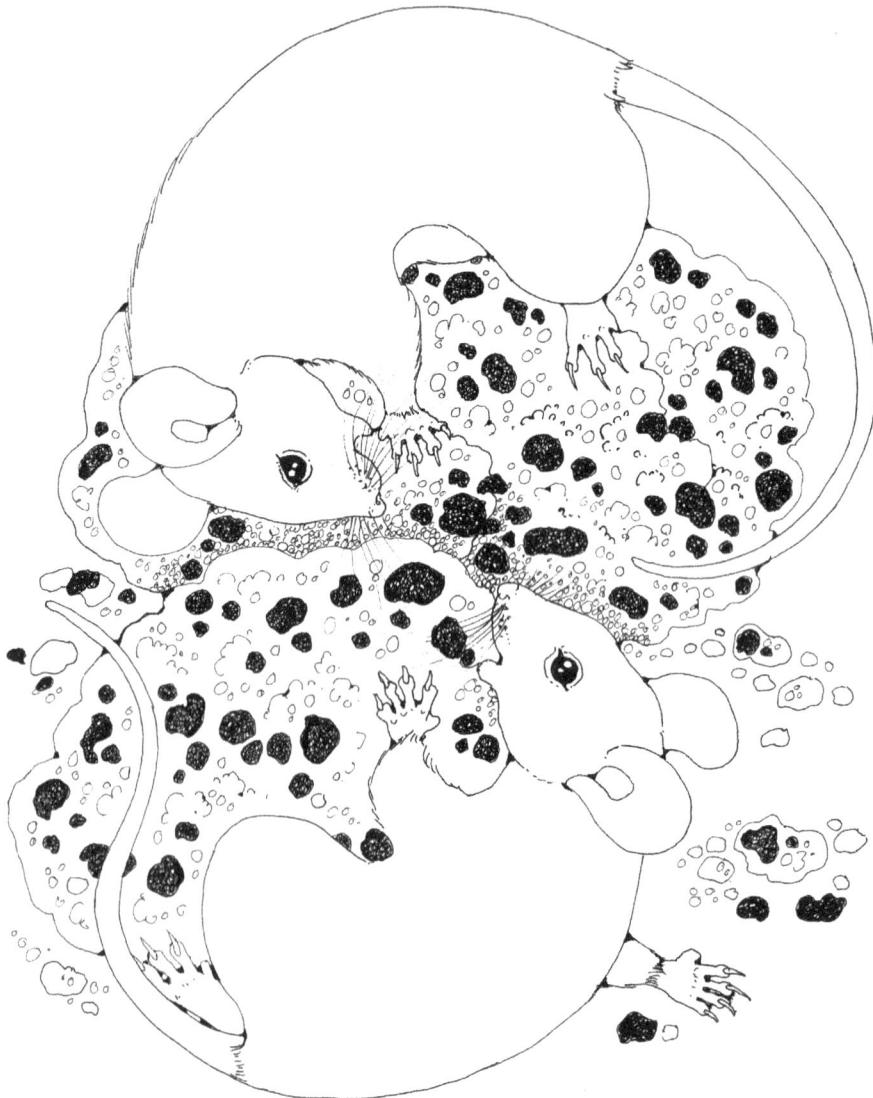

Cat Context

A friend who came
In from the wild,
A link
To times when
We were not so brave
And cowered in caves,
A cat to remind us who
We are
And how
We haven't come that far.

A Salutary Tale

Peck, peck, peck, CAW!
More, more, more!
The magpie's is a pesky chick,
The parent's sick of pick, pick, pick!

The grating cries that never cease,
This parent bird
Just wants some peace!
A hop away, another hop,
The well-fed hatchling
Will not stop!

The cat up on the garden wall
Sees it all.
One more hop, just out of reach,
The cat leaps…

End piece

A cat's derriere's
A swank affair,
The rhythmic sway,
A cat sashay!

Tail in air,
Not a care!
The curl's a
Rhetorical question mark.
Be warned,
If you're not 'in the know,'
Don't ask!

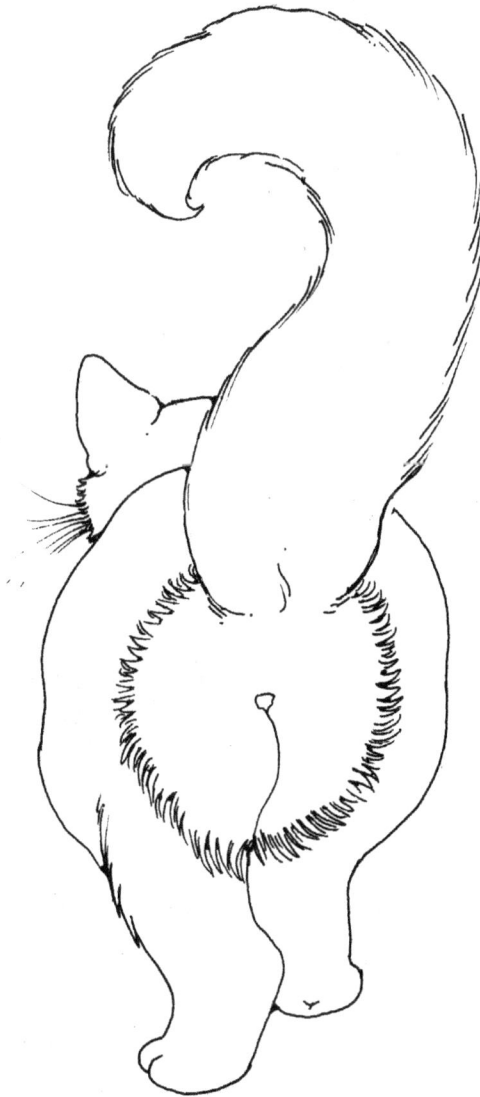

i

Tilly and Trixie – friendship, opposites, sharing.
Everyone's Cats and Someone – pet care, cat curfews, neighbourhood dynamics.
The Sea Cat Dreams – coping with change, grief, loss, change, farm life vs seafaring life vs coastal life.
Scaredy Who?! – medieval settings, living in medieval times vs modern living, fear, sound effects.
Funny Bones! – cats, dragons, risky behaviour, warnings, e.g. storm, flood and fire warnings, calm in face of threat vs panic behaviour, fire plan, cyclone season plan.
Mistress Mouse - Stranger danger, risk taking, mice, cats, predators, prey.
Good Reasons for Having a Cat - [1] cats, predators, pest control, [2] sharing resources, pets [3] intergenerational relationships, caring, pets [4] personal space, neighbourliness, respect, stray cats, lateral thinking.
Cat Context - breeding, domesticating wild animals, behaviour humans vs animals.
A Salutary Tale - risky behaviour, natural instincts, prey and predator.
End Piece – characteristics, traits, personality.

Acknowledgements

The Perfect Pet; Wild Ride with Fred; Pleas to Please; Living Dangerously; Take a Back Seat, in *Finding the Funny Bone,* KBS, 2006, Vol 6 in the series "Poetry Action for Classroom and Stage"

Abbie; Lean Cat Cuisine, in *Imagimals,* KBS, 2005 Vol 1 in the series "Poetry Action for Classroom and Stage"

Cat Curl, in *The Mozzie* edited by Gloria Benjamin Yates & Ron Heard

In the Shadow of the Heart in *Small Packages* edited by Rob Morris, vol.1

Of Catalumphs and Hippograffes; Her Majesty's Adviser, in *"Prints Rhyming Anthology,* edited by Sally Odgers, 2015

Biographical Note - Author

J.R.Poulter once worked in a circus. This definitely qualifies her to write for children! She has been published in Australia, UK and USA, having 30 books with mainstream publishers, including major award winner "Mending Lucille," and more digital books. "Poetry Action for Classroom and Stage" is her 6 volume series for education. More books are coming...

J.R. loves inspiring folk of all ages with her passion for poetry and prose and the fun to be had with words. Her workshops and dramatised readings have enthused all age groups, literally from one to 100!

In collaboration with Craig Smith, she created a picture book for an enthusiastic, participatory audience for the Lockyer Festival. Under the name of J.R.McRae, she also writes novels (including YA), literary poetry and short stories, as well as doing photography and artwork .

Her latest venture, under both writing names, consists of global collaborations with over 50 illustrators and designers from over 20 countries.

Websites:

http://www.wordwings.wix.com/publishing

Follow us on Facebook
https://www.facebook.com/Cattitudes.Cattiverse/?ref=br_rs

J. R. McRae
CATS'
EYES

Illustration:
Vasilis Grivas

Cuddle Kitten
and
Puddle Pup

by: J. R. Poulter

illustrated by: Trish Flannery

RaaYHhHhRrrr!

By J. R. Poulter
Illustrated by Mandy Sinclair

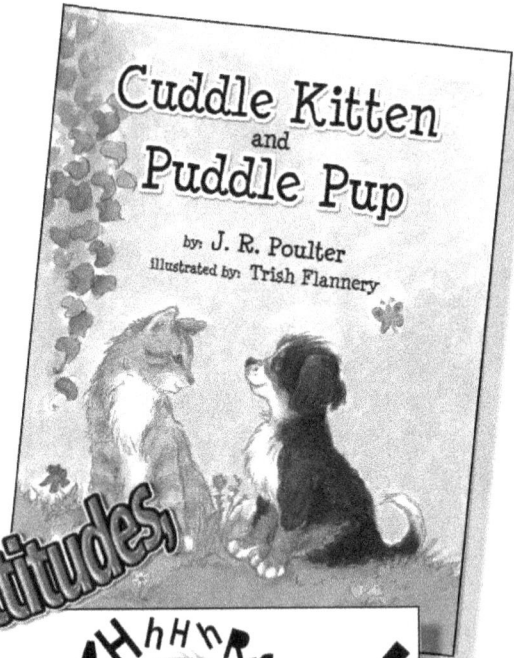

If you enjoyed Cattitudes,
you might like –

Cats' Eyes,
Cuddle Kitten & Puddle Pup,
Raaaahhhhrrrr!
The Sea Cat Dreams
are all available from
www.wordwings.wix.com

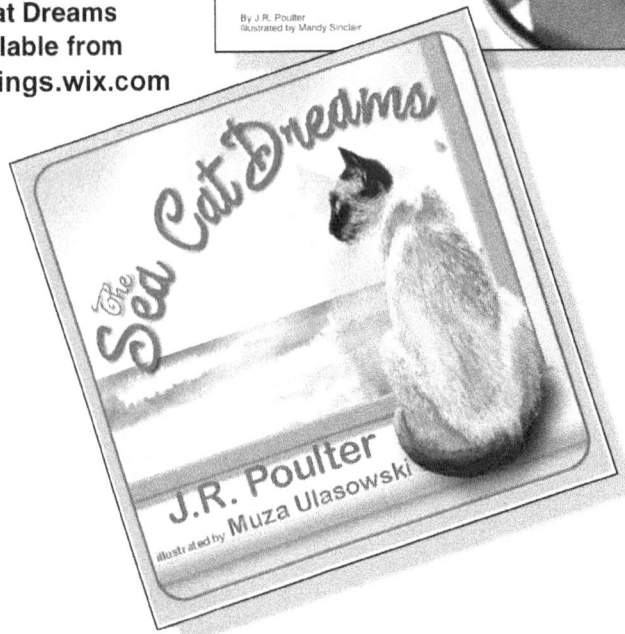

The Sea Cat Dreams

J.R. Poulter

illustrated by Muza Ulasowski

Biographical Note – Illustrator

Dandi Palmer has been an illustrator for over thirty five years, mainly of educational books. Her work also includes commissions by the Radio Times, Prima, UNESCO, BBC Focus and many more publications.

Recent books are *How to Draw Dinosaurs* and *How to Draw Insects* for the Search Press.

www.dandipal.uk has a selection of picture books as well as samples of other illustrations and portfolio of published work.

Since 1984 four adult science fiction novels have been published under the name of Jane Palmer.

A collection of colouring books for all ages by
Dandi Palmer, and published by Dodo Books,
can be found at
www.booksfromdodo.uk

Sample pages from the **Pictures to Colour In** series.

More books
from
Dandi Palmer

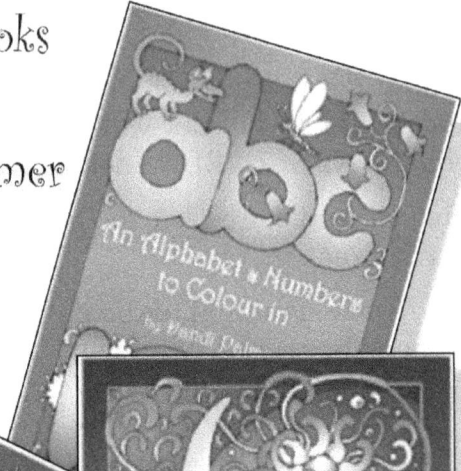

Pictures to
Colour in
by Dandi Palmer

abc
An Alphabet & Numbers
to Colour in
by Dandi Palmer

Pictures
to Colour in 3
by Dandi Palmer

Fantasy Pictures
to Colour in
by Dandi Palmer

**Colouring Books
available from
Amazon**

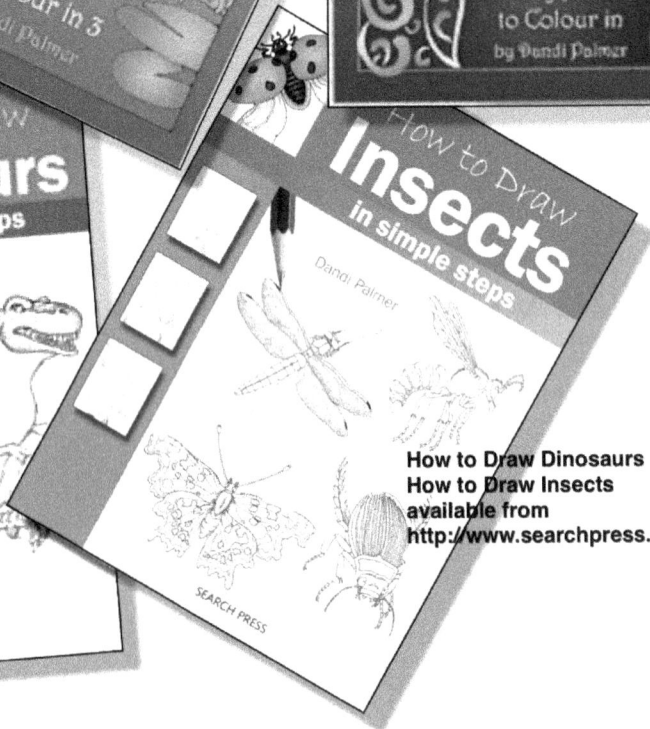

How to Draw
Dinosaurs
in simple steps

Dandi Palmer

SEARCH PRESS

How to Draw
Insects
in simple steps

Dandi Palmer

SEARCH PRESS

**How to Draw Dinosaurs &
How to Draw Insects
available from
http://www.searchpress.com**

SUBJECT INDEX

www.ingramcontent.com/pod-product-compliance
Lightning Source LLC
Chambersburg PA
CBHW081545040426
42448CB00015B/3228